DC COMICS™ SUPER HEROES

HOW TO DRAW SUPERMAN™

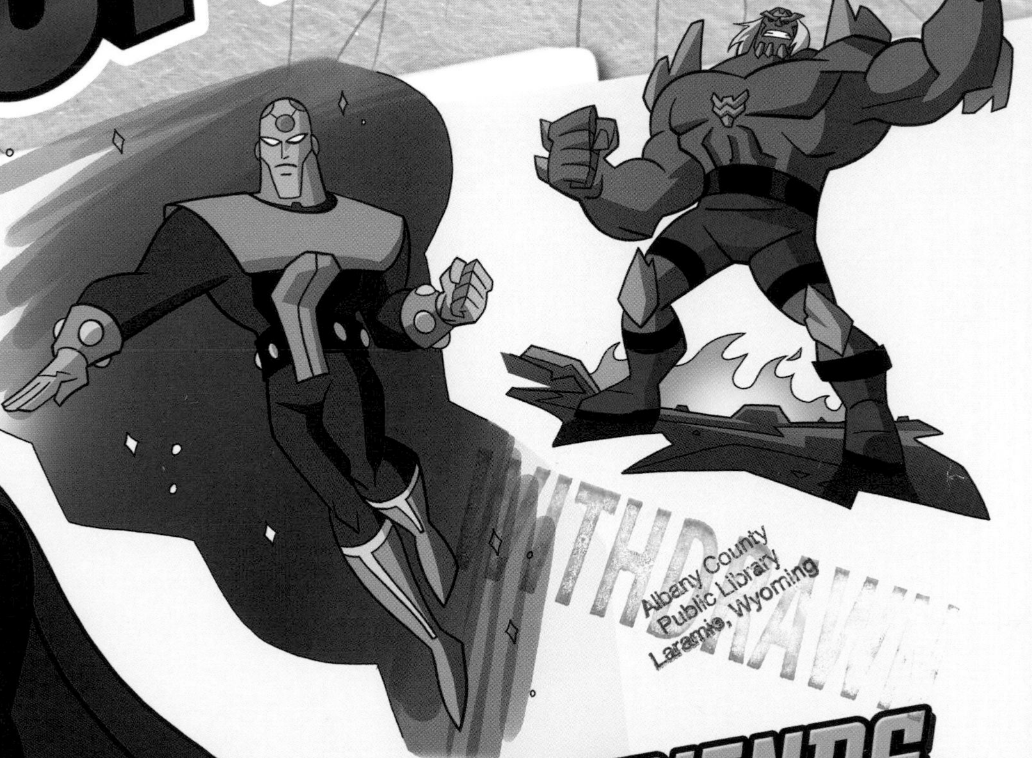

AND HIS FRIENDS AND FOES

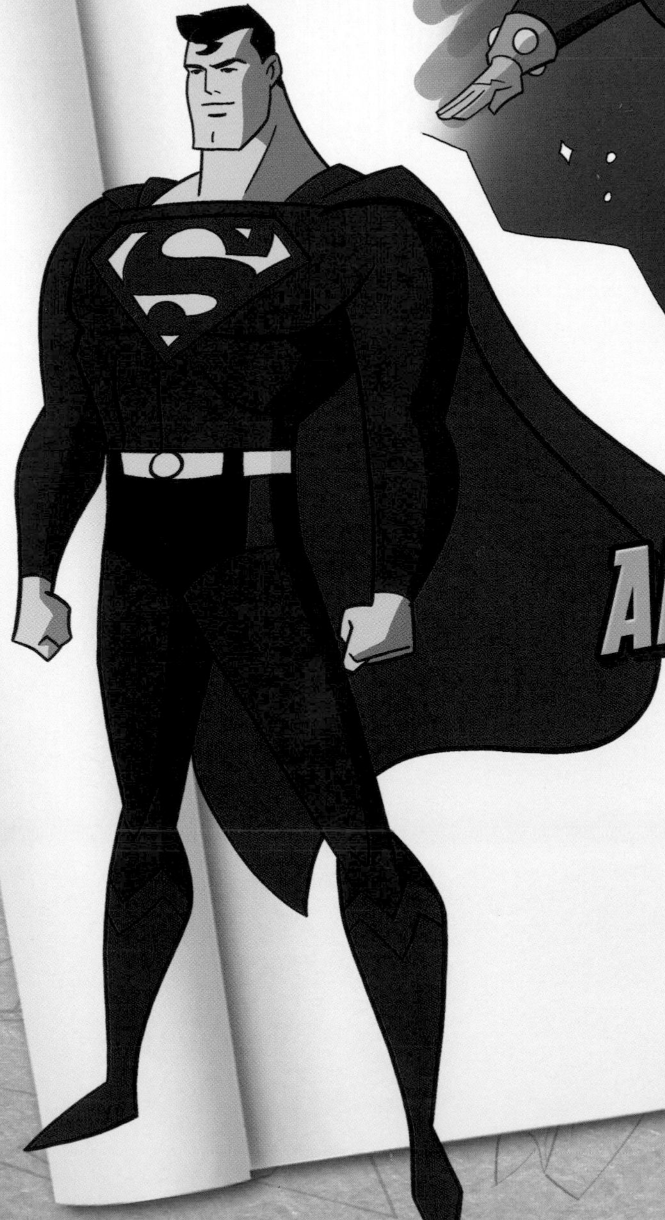

by Aaron Sautter
illustrated by Erik Doescher

Superman created by Jerry Siegel and Joe Shuster
By Special Arrangement with the Jerry Siegel Family

CAPSTONE PRESS
a capstone imprint

Published in 2015 by Capstone Press,
a Capstone Imprint
1710 Roe Crest Drive
North Mankato, Minnesota 56003
www.capstonepub.com

Library of Congress Cataloging-in-Publication Data
Sautter, Aaron.
How to draw Superman and his friends and foes / by Aaron Sautter, illustrated by Erik Doescher.
pages cm.—(DC Super heroes. Drawing DC super heroes)
Summary: "Simple step-by-step instructions teach readers how to draw Superman and
his friends and enemies"—Provided by publisher.
ISBN 978-1-4914-2156-7 (library binding)
1. Cartoon characters—Juvenile literature. 2. Superman (Fictitious character)—Juvenile literature.
3. Drawing—Technique—Juvenile literature. I. Doescher, Erik. II. Title.
NC1764.8.H47S285 2015
741.5'1—dc23   2014023862

Credits
Designer: Ted Williams
Art Director: Nathan Gassman
Production Specialist: Kathy McColley

Design Elements
Capstone Studio: Karon Dubke; Shutterstock: Artishok, Bennyartist, Eliks, gst, Mazzzur, Roobcio

Printed in the United States of America in North Mankato, Minnesota.
092014   008482CGS15

DRAWING PROJECTS

LET'S DRAW THE MAN OF STEEL!

Some people call him the Last Son of Krypton or the Man of Steel. But whatever people call him, one thing remains true—Superman is the first and most powerful super hero of them all.

Superman was born as Kal-El on the planet Krypton. However, he didn't grow up there. His parents, Jor-El and Lara Lor-Van, knew that Krypton was about to be destroyed. To save their baby son, they sent him to Earth in a special spacecraft. When young Kal landed near Smallville, Kansas, he was found by Jonathan and Martha Kent. The loving couple named him Clark and raised him as their own son.

As Clark grew he learned that he had many amazing abilities. Earth's yellow sun gave him powers such as super-strength and speed, heat vision, flight, and bulletproof skin. As an adult Clark chose to use his powers to defend the Earth and protect its people. He became Superman, the Man of Steel!

Welcome to the world of Superman! On the following pages you'll learn to draw Superman, his friends, and several of his most powerful enemies.

Let your imagination soar and see what kind of Superman drawings you can create yourself!

WHAT YOU'LL NEED

You don't need superpowers to draw mighty heroes. But you'll need some basic tools. Gather the following supplies before starting your awesome art.

PAPER: You can get special drawing paper from art supply and hobby stores. But any type of blank, unlined paper will work fine.

PENCILS: Drawings should always be done in pencil first. Even the pros use them. If you make a mistake, it'll be easy to erase and redo it. Keep plenty of these essential drawing tools on hand.

PENCIL SHARPENER: To make clean lines, you need to keep your pencils sharp. Get a good pencil sharpener. You'll use it a lot.

ERASERS: As you draw, you're sure to make mistakes. Erasers give artists the power to turn back time and erase those mistakes. Get some high quality rubber or kneaded erasers. They'll last a lot longer than pencil erasers.

BLACK MARKER PENS: When your drawing is ready, trace over the final lines with black marker pen. The dark lines will help make your characters stand out on the page.

COLORED PENCILS AND MARKERS: Ready to finish your masterpiece? Bring your characters to life and give them some color with colored pencils or markers.

SUPERMAN'S SUIT

When Clark arrived on Earth from Krypton, he was wrapped in blue and red blankets. Martha Kent used the blankets to create Superman's suit and cape. The Man of Steel doesn't wear a mask with his outfit. He wants to earn people's trust and show that he has nothing to hide.

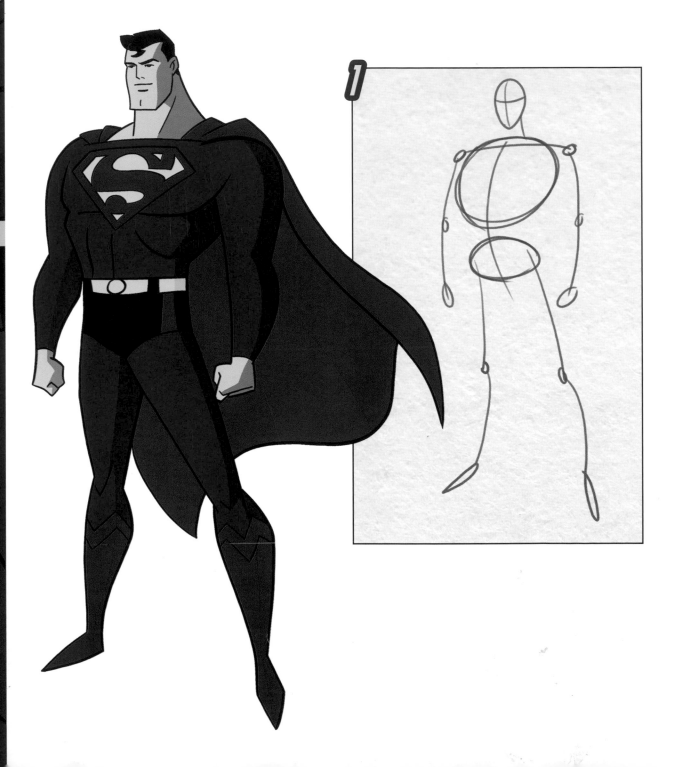

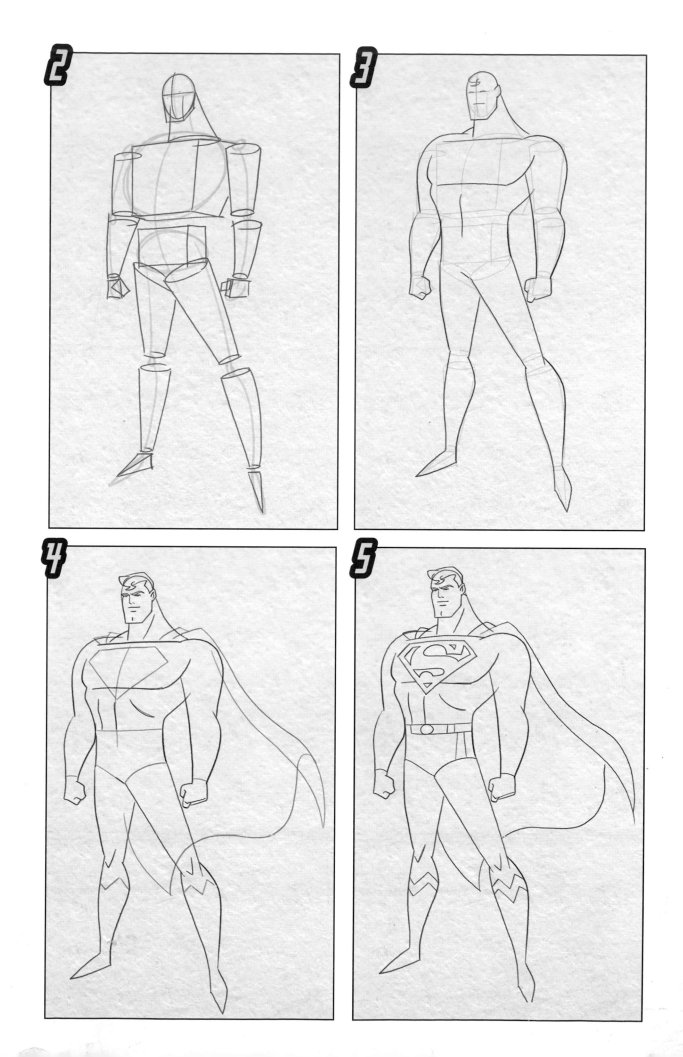

FORTRESS OF SOLITUDE

Superman normally calls Metropolis home. But when he needs time to himself, he goes to his secret Fortress of Solitude in the Arctic. There is only one door into the fortress, which is always locked. Only Superman has the strength needed to lift the giant metal key that unlocks the fortress door.

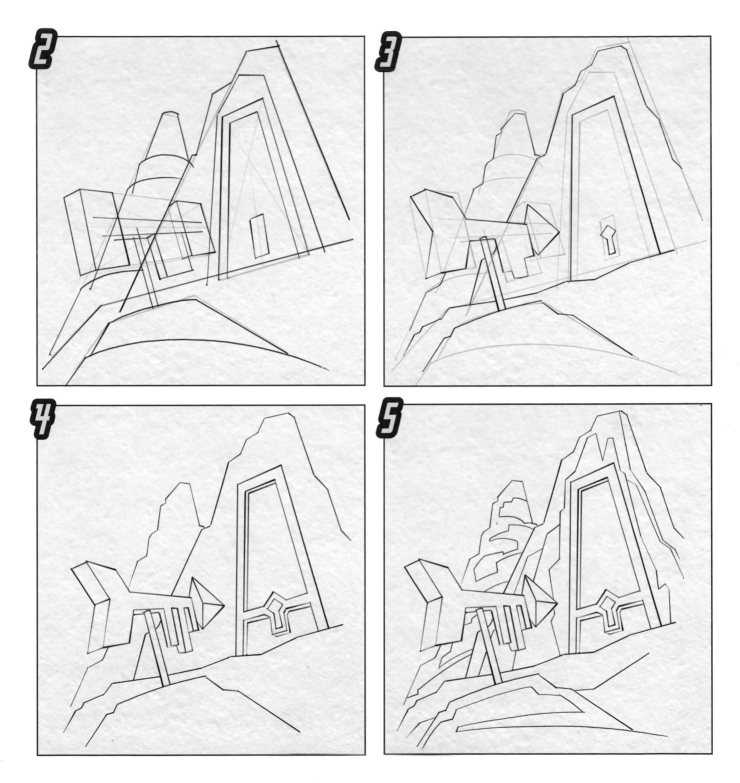

DRAWING IDEA
Next try to draw Superman lifting the key to open the Fortress door!

1

HEAT VISION

Heat vision is one of Superman's most powerful and useful abilities. He can use it to smash rocks or blast through concrete walls. Superman can also focus this power and use it like a laser beam. He often uses this ability to cut through steel plates or weld objects together to save people in danger.

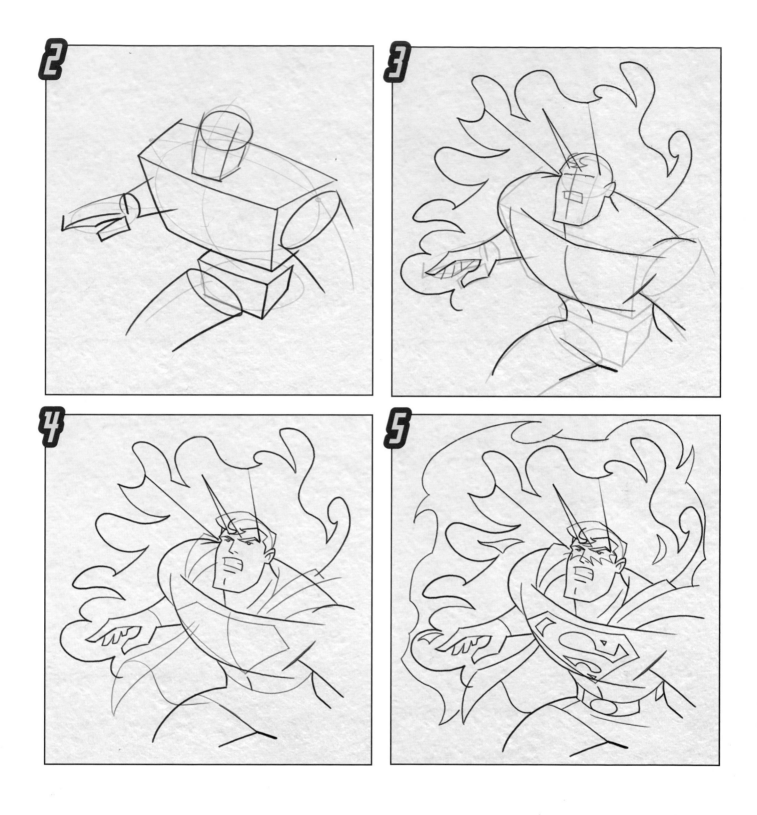

DRAWING IDEA
Try drawing Superman blasting through a rock wall with his heat vision!

DEFENDING EARTH

Threats to Earth and its people don't always come from villains'
evil plans. Superman stays alert for natural disasters and threats
from space too. When an asteroid is on course to hit Earth, the
Man of Steel is ready. He flies into space to meet it head-on. With
one swing of his mighty fist, he can smash the rock to bits and
keep it from slamming into the planet.

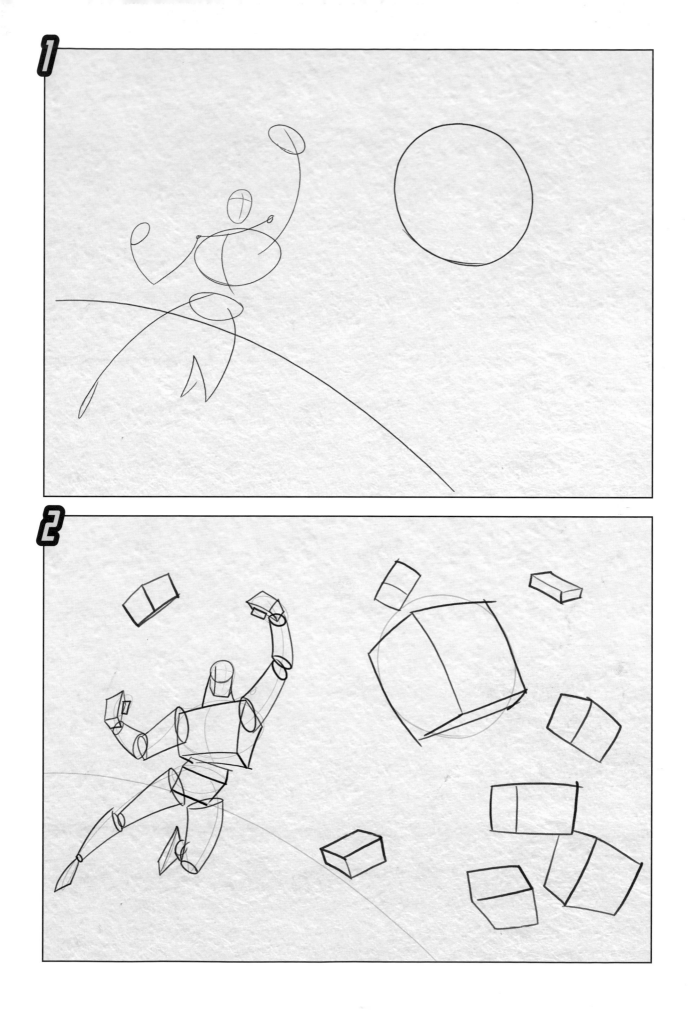

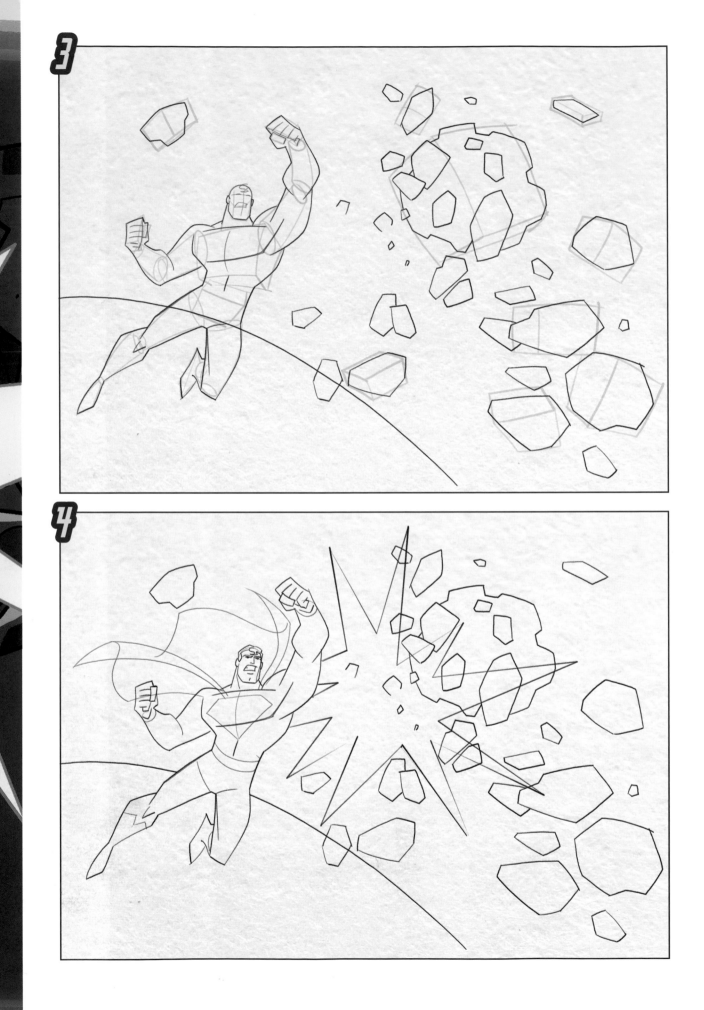

DAILY PLANET FRIENDS

Names: Lois Lane and Jimmy Olsen

Home Base: *Daily Planet* Building, Metropolis

Occupation: reporter; photographer

Abilities: strong investigation skills

Background:
Everybody needs a few good friends, including the Man of Steel. Clark's closest friends work with him at the *Daily Planet*. Jimmy is a photographer and often gets the best photos of Superman. Lois works closely with Clark to cover the biggest news stories in Metropolis.

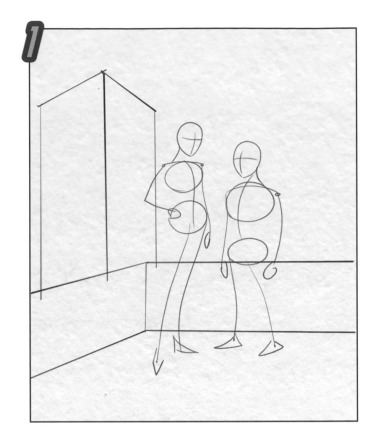

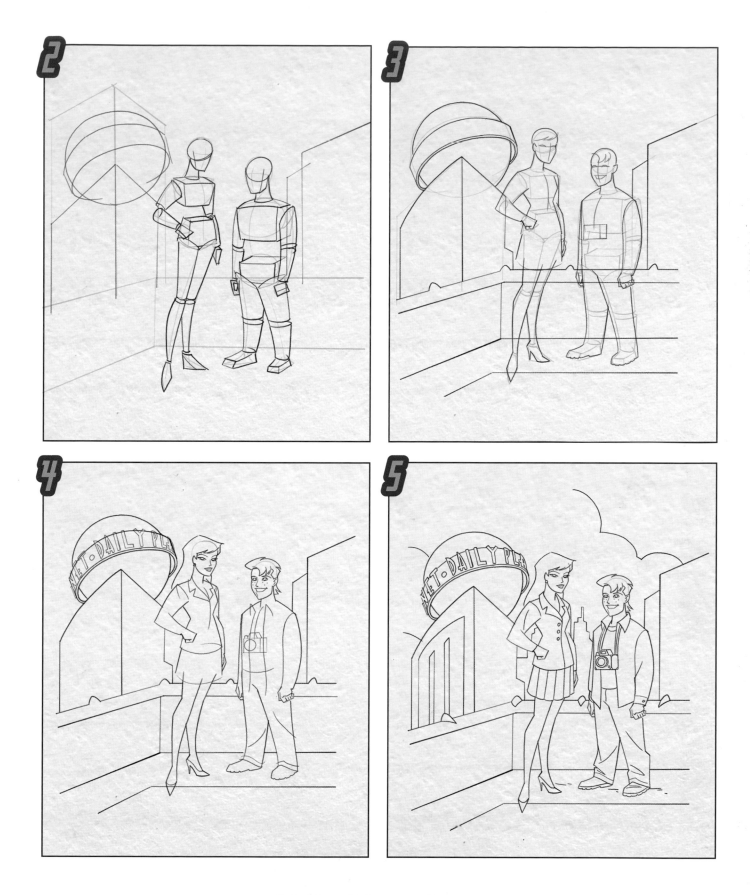

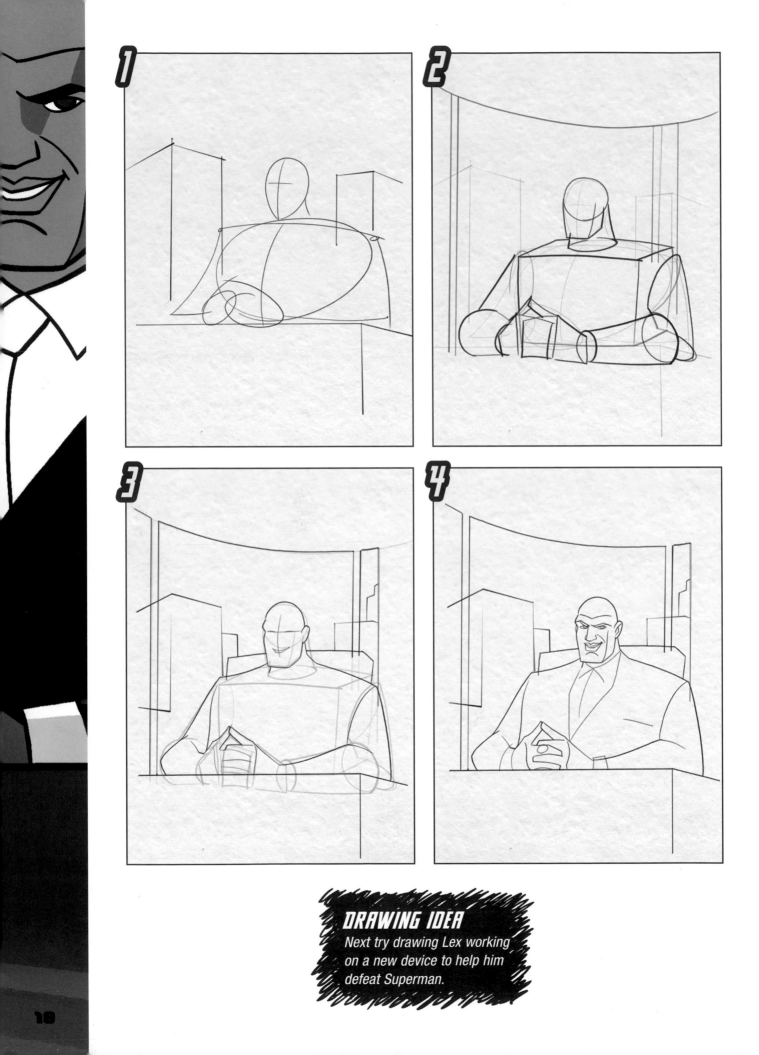

1

2

3

4

DRAWING IDEA
Next try drawing Lex working on a new device to help him defeat Superman.

LEX LUTHOR

Real Name: Alexander "Lex" Luthor

Home Base: LexCorp, Metropolis

Occupation: successful businessman, criminal mastermind

Enemy of: Superman

Abilities: scientific genius

Background: Lex Luthor is one of the richest and most powerful people in Metropolis. But Superman knows Lex's dirty secret—that he gained most of his wealth through crime. Lex is always careful not to get caught breaking the law red-handed. Lex doesn't have superpowers. However, he has invented several amazing electronic devices to help him succeed in his criminal activities.

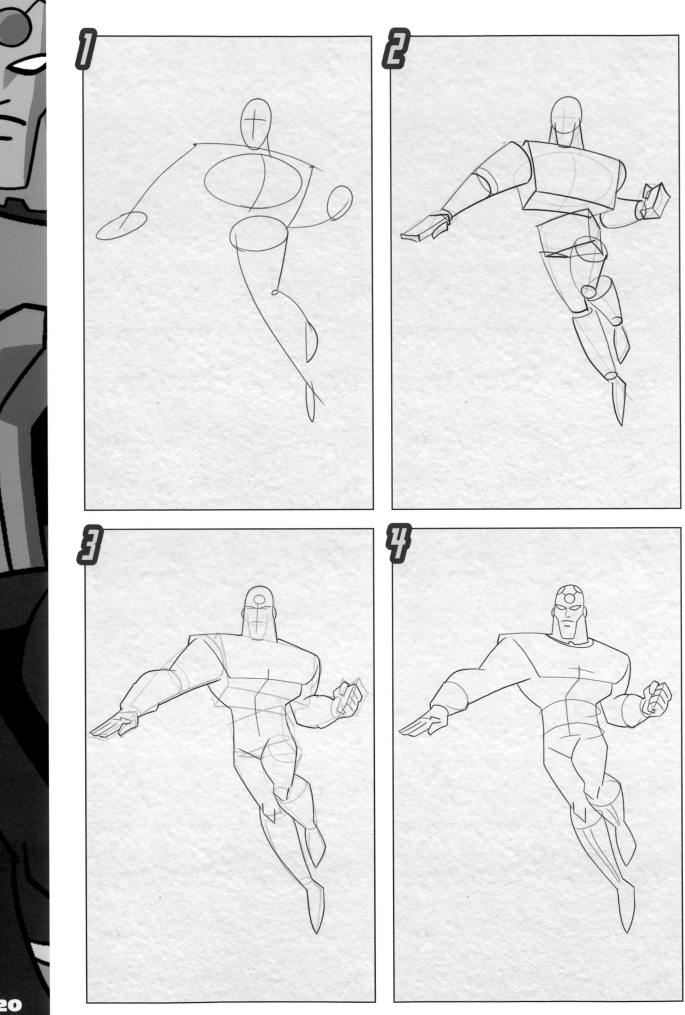

BRAINIAC

Real Name: unknown

Home Base: Skull Ship

Occupation: super-villain

Enemy of: Superman

Abilities: genius intelligence, enhanced strength, flight, master of technology

Background: Brainiac was once a powerful computer on Krypton. It became so intelligent that it became self-aware and left the planet before it was destroyed. Now Brainiac travels the universe, destroying countless planets to harvest their technologies. Brainiac can take control of most forms of technology and uses its vast knowledge to outsmart anyone who stands in its way. Only Superman can match the wits and strength of the walking, talking computer.

DRAWING IDEA
Next try drawing Brainiac's powerful skull-shaped spaceship!

BIZARRO

Real Name: unknown

Home Base: Bizarro World

Occupation: super-villain

Enemy of: Superman

Abilities: super-strength, flight, freeze vision, fire breath

Background: Bizarro is a twisted clone of Superman created by Lex Luthor. Bizarro's powers are equal yet opposite to Superman's. For example, instead of fiery heat vision, Bizarro blasts beams of ice from his eyes. He is also unpredictable and doesn't know his own strength, making him a dangerous threat to Metropolis.

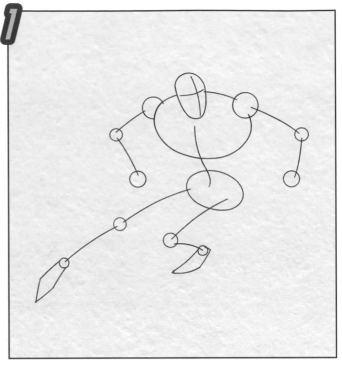

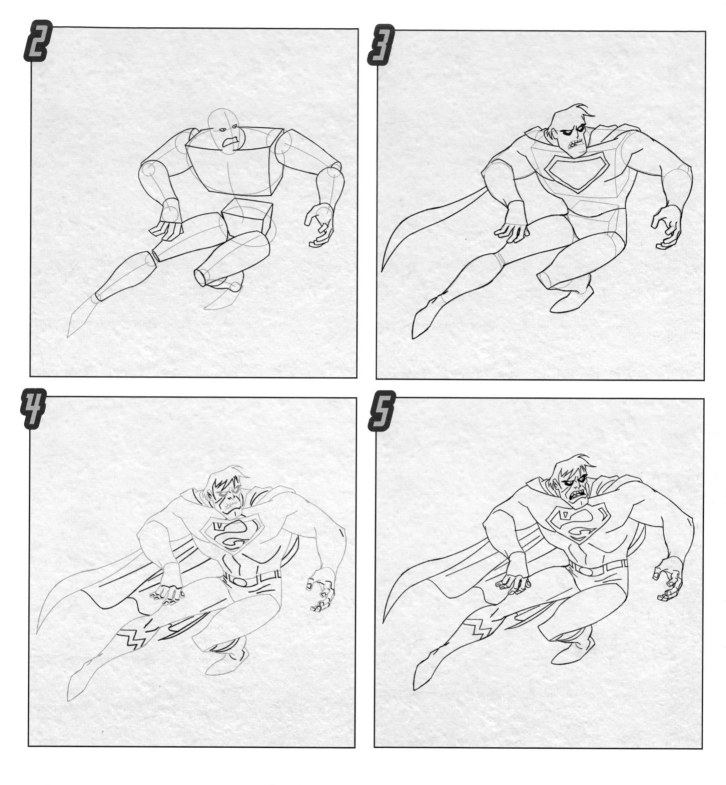

DRAWING IDEA
Try drawing Bizarro saving a cat stuck in a tree—by pulling the tree out of the ground!

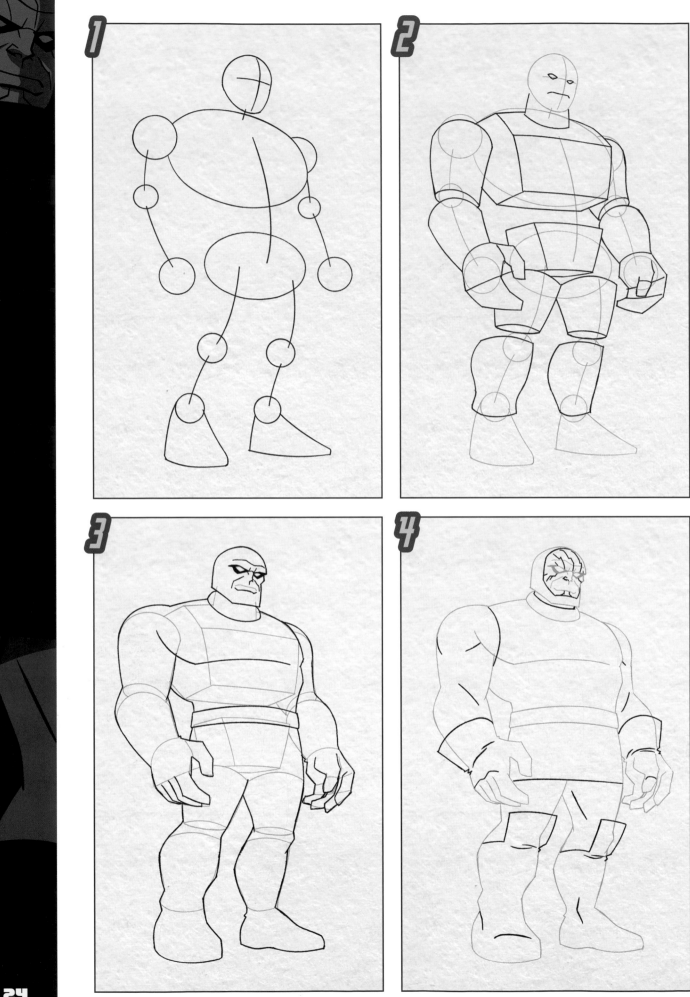

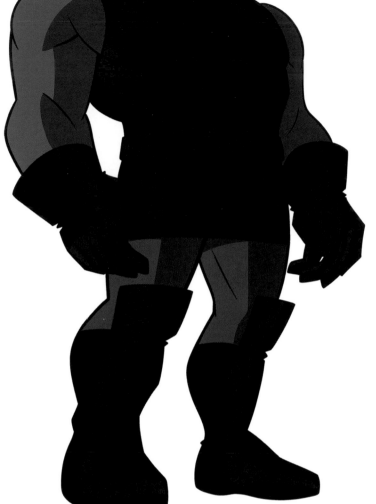

DARKSEID

Real Name: Uxas

Home Base: Apokolips

Occupation: dictator and tyrant, New God

Enemy of: Superman

Abilities: superhuman strength, speed, and stamina; invulnerability; immortality; genius intellect; telepathy; mind control; Omega Beams

Background: Darkseid rules over the planet Apokolips with an iron fist. But he also aims to rule the entire universe! Darkseid has limitless strength and can blast his enemies with deadly Omega Beams from his eyes. Only Superman has the strength to truly weaken or injure him. With his unmatched power, Darkseid is nothing less than the most dangerous enemy in the known universe.

DRAWING IDEA
Next draw Darkseid as he tries to defeat the Man of Steel with his deadly Omega Beams!

DOOMSDAY

Real Name: Doomsday

Home Base: Krypton

Occupation: destroyer

Enemy of: Superman

Abilities: super-strength and speed, regeneration, invincibility

Background: Doomsday is an indestructible force of rage. He desires only to destroy everything in his path. The creature is nearly impossible to stop. If he dies, he just comes back to life stronger than before—and is also immune to whatever killed him! Doomsday's body is covered with sharp, jagged bones that he uses as both armor and dangerous weapons. His superpowers and violent nature make Doomsday one of the Man of Steel's deadliest foes.

DRAWING IDEA
After drawing Doomsday, try drawing him in a major battle with the Man of Steel!

GENERAL ZOD

Real Name: Dru-Zod

Home Base: Krypton

Occupation: criminal warlord

Enemy of: Superman

Abilities: super-strength, speed, and breath; heat vision; flight; invincibility

Background: General Zod was a military leader who tried to take over Krypton, but failed. As punishment Zod and his followers were banished to the mysterious Phantom Zone. When they escaped, Zod decided that he would rule over Earth instead of Krypton. Luckily Superman is there to stop Zod and his evil plans. However, Zod's powers match those of Superman. Defeating this warrior from Krypton will be the Man of Steel's greatest challenge.

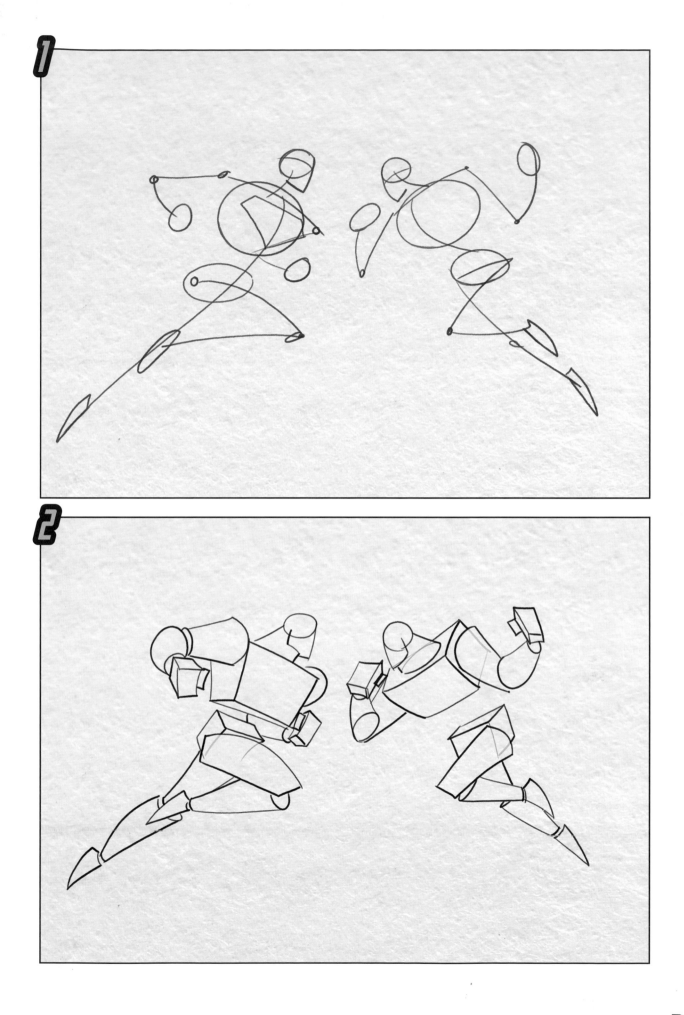

1

2

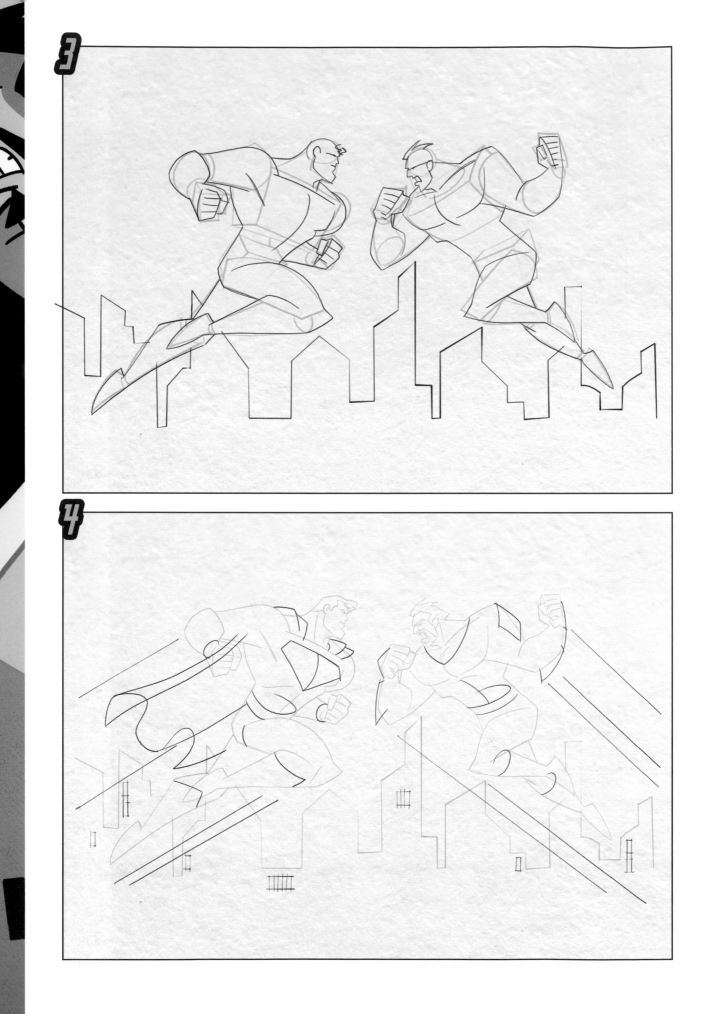

INTERNET SITES

FactHound offers a safe, fun way to find Internet sites related to this book.
All of the sites on FactHound have been researched by our staff.

Here's all you do:

Visit *www.facthound.com*

Type in this code: 9781491421567

Check out projects, games and lots more at
www.capstonekids.com

TITLES IN THIS SET